Building Self-Esteem
5 Steps: How To Feel
"Good Enough" About Yourself

Building Self-Esteem
5 Steps: How To Feel
"Good Enough" About Yourself

THE RELATIONSHIP FORMULA WORKBOOK SERIES

Jill P. Weber PhD

ISBN: 1535295279
ISBN 13: 9781535295277
Library of Congress Control Number: 2016912108
CreateSpace Independent Publishing Platform
North Charleston, South Carolina

About the Author

Jill P. Weber, PhD, is a clinical psychologist in private practice in Washington, DC. She is the author of *Having Sex, Wanting Intimacy: Why Women Settle for One-Sided Relationships*. She writes a relationship and self-esteem blog for *Psychology Today*. Her writing has appeared in the *Huffington Post, Healthy Living Magazine*, and *USA Today*, and she is a psychology contributor to various media outlets including the *Washington Post, Nightline*, CNN, Discovery Channel, and the Associated Press.

The Relationship Formula Workbook Series

1. *Breaking Up & Divorce 5 Steps: How to Heal and Be Comfortable Alone*
2. *Building Self-Esteem 5 Steps: How to Feel "Good Enough" about Yourself*
3. *Toxic Love 5 Steps: How to Identify Toxic-Love Patterns and Find Fulfilling Attachments*
4. *Getting Close to Others 5 Steps: How to Develop Intimate Relationships and Still Be True to Yourself*

Contents

Preface

Many of the people I work with in my psychotherapy practice have to build up their nerve to confess to me that they have "self-esteem issues." They are ashamed of these feelings and believe they are at fault for the situation. They tell me, "I know there is something very off about me, but I can't quite figure out what," or "I have a bad feeling inside of me all the time," or "I never liked myself, even as a child." They commonly ask questions like "What's wrong with me?" and "Am I too flawed to have a healthy relationship?" Many people tolerate these corrosive thoughts on a daily and even hourly basis. Some fall so frequently into spirals of self-doubt and self-hatred that they no longer realize they are doing it.

If you're not feeling good enough about yourself, then you likely replay negative-thought streams in your head, each painful memory or thought opening the door to the next, producing a never-ending stream of self-doubt and feelings of worthlessness. When you realize what you are doing, you may then harshly criticize yourself for thinking this way, which triggers a new bout of negative thinking and despair.

Neuroscientists give us the reason for why people become stuck in this downward spiral. We each have a neuronal network that may or may not reflect reality. This network guides our judgment about ourselves. It tells us if we are capable, lovable, and effective—or not.

If while you were growing up, your parents, teachers, or peers were regularly critical of you, or you were made to feel cast out or different in some way, then your sense of yourself may be based on feeling unworthy and not good enough. Each time you have a setback or feel vulnerable, your brain pulls up this negative self-image and triggers a series of similarly negative thoughts.

If you struggle with not feeling good enough, it may be hard for you to fully take in the experience when good things do happen to you. Positive experiences do not match your well-worn neuronal pattern that tells you that you are inadequate. This condition has the power to influence every aspect of a person's life and decision-making process.

And at the same time, people who struggle with self-esteem also tend to put a great deal of pressure on themselves to make "right" and "correct" choices. They may think and overthink, yet take no actionable steps to solve the problems at hand—*analysis by paralysis* sets in. Feeling as if you are spinning your wheels but getting nowhere adds fodder for self-criticism. Overanalyzing and criticizing yourself creates an overwhelming sense of powerlessness and helplessness.

Outsourcing Self-Esteem to Relationships

People who struggle with feeling good enough tend to use relationships as a crutch or drug, so to speak, to find a modicum of peace. As they founder in a sea of self-doubt and self-critical thinking, a new relationship or love interest may feel like a life preserver.

Perhaps you have had an underlying belief that you are not good enough. To compensate for this belief, you have found yourself becoming extremely focused on gaining the love of others. Perhaps you put so much energy into winning this love that you have left yourself exhausted, not knowing who you are and what you want. A person who avoids feelings of worthlessness by working overtime to win the approval of others can't succeed because self-doubt and even self-hatred always sabotage personal relationships.

Low self-esteem also leaves people vulnerable to something I refer to as *sextimacy*, which is using sex as a way to gain validation. Of course when romantic attachment is based on sextimacy, the immediate rush of a new relationship and temporary connection soon wear off, and the inadequate self comes roaring back in. I explore sextimacy in detail in my book *Having Sex, Wanting Intimacy—Why Women Settle For One-Sided Relationships*.

If you struggle with not feeling good enough to get what you want out of life, then you very likely also have a belief that this feeling of inadequacy is immutable. The key to lifting the veil of self-doubt and blocking negative-thinking spirals that take you nowhere is realizing that you can change this way of thinking about yourself.

Becoming Unstuck

The encouraging news is that neuroscience research shows that the brain will adapt and grow through something called *neuronal plasticity*. Athletes, musicians, and meditative monks have increased the capacity of their brains for specialized pursuits. The brain changes when it is made to work repeatedly at something new. The process by which one develops low self-esteem is the same process that will undo your negative self-image. Positive change will come by repeatedly engaging with new life experiences.

You may be saying to yourself, "Okay, I get it, but I don't want to do this. It's too much work, time, and effort." Nevertheless, know that change is possible. Instead of being swamped by a dark flood of negative thinking and bad feelings about yourself, let's step back and consider who you are—flaws and all.

Knowing yourself and how your mind ticks does not mean you like everything about yourself, but if you allow it, it can mean you accept how it functions. This acceptance opens the door to finding ways around the self-defeating aspects of your thinking. The exercises in this workbook, if done consistently, will help realign your negative self-perception. And too, having a more positive self-perception will tremendously improve your relationship choices and the quality of your interpersonal interactions.

I plucked my soul out of its secret place,
And held it to the mirror of my eye,
To see it like a star against the sky,
A twitching body quivering in space,
A spark of passion shining on my face.
And I explored it to determine why
This awful key to my infinity

Conspires to rob me of sweet joy and grace.
And if the sign may not be fully read,
If I can comprehend but not control,
I need not gloom my days with futile dread,
Because I see a part and not the whole.
Contemplating the strange, I'm comforted
By this narcotic thought: I know my soul.
"I KNOW MY SOUL," BY CLAUDE MCKAY

Special note: Keep a notebook handy so you can write down your answers to the exercises in this workbook. Review the notebook from time to time to remind yourself what you are learning about yourself as you grow through this program. The more you review the material, the more the tools you've been practicing will become automatic.

STEP 1

Take Stock of What You Won't Accept about Yourself

You know what it's like when you just can't get a particular song out of your head? People who have low self-esteem feel as if they have no control over what comes into their minds. The same poisonous thoughts just keep playing over and over.

Take the example of Jenny. Jenny walked into most of her social situations and other life events carrying an inferiority complex. She always felt like she was out of step with the group, and therefore, she acted in a self-effacing way, hoping to minimize exposing her lack of social rhythm. People barely noticed her because she successfully minimized herself.

Jenny was not aware of her inferiority complex or how it promoted her self-effacing behavior. What she did know was every time she had to deal with a new group, handle a conflict, or struggle to have her needs met, she invariably felt frustrated and, paradoxically, minimized. At the conclusion of an event, she was depleted and felt hopeless about fulfilling her goals. A self-critical dialogue would play out again, setting her up to walk into the next event with the same feelings of inferiority, thus repeating the pattern.

The first step in breaking the spiral of self-criticism and self-doubt that contributes to unfulfilling romantic and other relationships is to actually confront what it is you don't like about yourself.

Problem: "I can't bear to face what I don't like about myself."
Cure: Break up your low self-esteem complex into manageable pieces.

What I'm asking you to do may prompt anxiety or even panic. After all, perhaps one of the ways you have coped with feeling badly about yourself is that you've tried with all your might to stop thinking about it, or you've distracted yourself with other activities. Some people are so unsettled by the prospect of looking at what they fear or honestly feel about themselves that that they will go to destructive lengths to avoid it—including drug and alcohol abuse or the continuation of abusive relationship patterns. However, until you look at what you fear head on, you will continue in the same patterns of inadequacy and self-doubt that will not bring contentment.

A *special note about relationships:* If you do not feel good enough about yourself, you may be vulnerable to what I call the *illusion of fusion*, which means that you use others, romantic partners in particular, to fill a depleted you. If you have a negative self-image, you may be working tirelessly to find a cure by securing or sustaining a romantic attachment. As a result, you find yourself perpetually caught in a cycle of temporary highs followed by crushing lows. The history of these attachments can play out over a few hours or a much longer period of time. In either case, until self-love is present within, true love and care from outside will be fleeting.

If you fall into the illusion-of-fusion pattern, it's time to confront what it is that you don't like about yourself. You are probably saying, "What's to confront? I KNOW I don't like myself." But the reality for people who struggle with feelings of low self-worth is that they have lost touch with the specific thought streams and events that trigger these feelings. The exercises in this workbook are designed to help you get back in touch.

Perhaps you are thinking, "Everything makes me feel bad," and that may be true, but for most people, similar themes repeat. So it may be your physical appearance that makes you feel poorly, and this feels overwhelming because every few minutes, you are pinged with another negative thought about your body. As a client put it to me after doing a few of the exercises below, "Now that I see my patterns and what bothers me on paper, it's actually comforting. It feels more manageable in some way, like I can look at these specific things as problems instead of seeing my whole self as the problem."

First, we will consider the *types of situations* that make you feel poorly about yourself. Then we will consider *what it is you don't like about yourself*. And finally, we will take a look at the *thought streams* that tell you to feel poorly about yourself.

Exercise: Complete a Diary of What Makes You Feel Bad

Over the next week, write down the types of situations/events/people that trigger feelings of inferiority and inadequacy in you or that cause you to generally feel badly about yourself. If you prefer, imagine the experiences that typically trigger inadequate feelings or an internal sense of worthlessness.

Regarding the situations that trigger negative feelings about yourself, in your notebook, record answers to the following questions:

- At the time the negative feeling about yourself was triggered, what were you doing, or who were you around?

- What was the specific thing (whether words or actions) that brought on those negative feelings?

- What was the feeling generated? Sadness, shame, hurt, anxiety, embarrassment, disappointment, anger, or hopelessness?

- On a scale of zero to ten (ten being the strongest), how intense was the emotion for you?

- What did you do after the event? Did you hole up alone and isolate yourself, self-criticize, go out, exercise, drink alcohol, hook up, use drugs, or read a book?

As an example, Sara found that her feelings of inadequacy became more intense every time she was around her mother. She dreaded the visits beforehand, and then during their visits, she would go to painstaking lengths to appear as perfect as possible to keep her critical mother at bay. Nonetheless, every time they were around each other, her mother would make offhand critical comments about Sara's appearance, how much money she earned, or her romantic choices. She would say things like "I wish you would do something different with your hair," or "Have you thought about getting a real job YET?" or "Are you sure you want to eat THAT?" or "Have you gone to the gym lately?" Invariably, Sara left these encounters feeling helplessly bad, as if she were doing something wrong, and there was no way to fix it.

Sara persevered with her mother. She would plan future outings carefully, trying to be perfect and hoping it would go differently—all to no avail. Once she completed this diary, Sara became aware that her inadequacy was particularly triggered when she was around her mother and that she felt better about herself in other contexts. She realized the solution was not for her to be more perfect, but for her to draw clear boundaries with her mother. Over time, Sara became more and more comfortable telling her mother when she felt hurt or criticized. She often had to repeat the same lines over and over: "Mom, I know you mean well, but this particular conversation feels critical to me, and I no longer wish to talk about it." Eventually, her mother learned the limits of their relationship. Most importantly, Sara stopped the cycle of having her esteem pulled down by these encounters.

Exercise: Complete a Self-Loathing Inventory

Now let's turn to what it is *you* don't like about yourself. As much as possible, tune out everyone and everything else in your life—your work, your schooling, the people and situations you encounter—just focus on what you struggle with about yourself. I know it's hard to take a look, but it will help to actually write it down on paper.

Make two columns in your notebook. On the left side, write down each issue that makes you unhappy about yourself, and next to it, write down how long you have struggled with feeling negatively about that particular issue.

Now, which issues cause you the most suffering or preoccupy your thoughts the most? Rank them from zero (not upset at all) to ten (acute suffering). We will reference this list throughout the workbook.

Here are some sample items: "Stomach is too big," "Wrinkles," "Not assertive enough," "Not attractive enough," "Not smart," "Not ambitious," "Not fun enough," "Physically weak," "Don't make enough money," "Not in shape," "Fat," "No relationships," "Not enough relationships," "Poor diet," "Too much alcohol or drug usage," "Not sexually desirable," "Spouse/partner not good enough," "Breasts too small," and "Penis too small."

Exercise: Uncover Your Internal Critic

Another way to determine what you are doing to yourself that is causing pain is to consciously listen to your internal narrative. The internal narrator is that little voice in your head that is commenting and making observations about whatever it is you are experiencing in any particular moment. It's important that you begin to pay attention to your internal narrative and notice how it serves to help or to hinder you.

Sit somewhere quietly with no distractions. Call to mind one of the events from the diary exercise above or one of your self-loathing items. Concentrate on the event or item, bringing it to mind with great detail. Now tune into how your internal narrative is judging the particular item. What is it telling you about yourself? Is it critical, judgmental, or angry in tone? How does your internal narrative add to your insecurities or feelings of self-doubt?

Uncover the themes of your self-critical dialogue. Here are a few examples of common themes. See if your themes fall into one or more of these categories. After you read the examples, write down in your notebook a few sentences or even a paragraph about the nature of your internal dialogue.

- **The Failure Whisper:** Brian was so consumed with anxiety and the pressure to get things done that he was too busy to know what he felt about himself. When he settled down to hear that voice in his head, he realized it was making disparaging comments: "You screwed that up again," "You aren't as good as everyone else," "You are behind," "You'll never catch up," "Great, here we go again, making a fool out of ourselves," "You aren't doing anything right anymore," and "Life is passing you by." The only way he knew to silence the failure whisper was to work harder.

- **The Gremlin:** For Max, every time he felt as if things might be looking up in his romantic relationship or when he had an accomplishment of some sort at work, within an hour of his success, a voice in his head would remind him of something negative about himself: "You still haven't finished your master's degree," "You don't work out enough," "You're not attractive enough," "Don't forget that other project you need to finish," "You need to make more money," or "You need to work later/harder." The gremlin took away any period of pleasure or peace that might have followed a success.

- **The Forsaken:** For Liz, when someone let her down or when she hit a setback in her relationships, she felt terrifyingly alone. Her internal voice would say, "You are never going to be loved. You are different. There is something wrong with you that makes you unlovable." She was frightened that others would discover what she saw as a lamentable truth about herself. With this fear in mind, she worked hard to make connections and to keep everyone happy lest she have to hear the forsaken voice in her head.

- **Prudence:** Emily wanted to let go and have fun. She wanted to be spontaneous and in the moment with her friends and family. But each time she entered a new situation or was around social connections, the voice in her head reminded her of everything that could go wrong. She found herself consumed by inhibiting thoughts: "Watch out—don't say that. It might offend," "Don't dance. You'll look stupid," "Don't go swimming. You look terrible in a bathing suit," "What if he doesn't like you," and "This or that might go wrong, and then what." Prudence also replayed events to Emily, reminding her of what she did wrong or how she could have handled a situation differently: "You said that so poorly." "Your joke was NOT funny." "You made everyone feel weird." All of this internal back talk took Emily out of the moment, so that when she was appearing to have fun or appearing to do interesting things, she was actually in her head, cautiously analyzing and scrutinizing her every move.

- **The Killjoy:** Sean had trouble enjoying himself because he was completely sidelined by even the slightest setback. Whenever he hit a bump in the road, he would tell himself how everything was going to go poorly and how he would never meet his goal. For example, he once took an exciting trip to Tahiti with his partner. The two planned the trip for months and were looking forward to every moment together. The night before they left, however, Sean was up with a head cold. On the way to the airport, his cell phone stopped working. These two events set off an internal dialogue of misery and defeat. Sean kept repeating his woes to his partner: "I feel so sick. I'm not going to enjoy this trip," "The flight is so long. It's going to be awful," and "I can't use my cell, so work is going to be freaking out." Even after they made it to their destination and were a few days into their trip, Sean still could not shake the killjoy. Every moment of beauty or joy was tainted by his internal voice reminding him of the long flight back, the price of their expensive bungalow, or how he would never recover from the jet lag. The killjoy zapped Sean's pleasure.

Exercise: Connect Your Self-loathing Thoughts to Your Narrative

Now review your responses to the last three exercises. Can you put together the themes of your responses? For example, perhaps work meetings trigger a failure-whisper dialogue because you feel you have never been as smart as those you admire, and you beat yourself up about your perceived failures and setbacks. Alternatively, perhaps meeting new people or fighting with your romantic partner triggers intense anxiety because deep down you believe you are unlovable, and if this is true, you are terrified of what your life alone will be like.

Write down the ways your negative-thought streams, events, and self-loathing items connect, and recognize the nature of the themes that, for you, repeat.

Instead of feeling as if your whole life is running amuck, are you starting to see that there are particular areas of your thinking that need to be tweaked? Recognize that if you continue to avoid examining the specific triggers for your feelings of inadequacy, the negative feelings you carry will perpetually get in the way of achieving what you want out of life.

You are a container; there is room for negative-thought streams and feelings to be present without requiring you to attack yourself. In this moment, try to connect with how long you have harbored these ways of thinking, and weigh how much pain this has likely brought to you. Show yourself that you are strong enough to face the negatives head on and that you don't need to live in fear. It's the pushing away that perpetuates low self-esteem.

There is a misperception that some people in the world are perfect or feel perfect all of the time; for most (if not all), this is not a realistic perception. What you can strive for is accepting yourself, as you are, warts and all, while at the same time believing that with effort you can improve and get more enjoyment from your life. You are changing the dynamics of your life by showing yourself that you can actually make room in a meaningful and compassionate way for what hurts and upsets you. Perfection always eludes, but a light heart and an open mind to life's possibilities do not require perfection.

Problem: "Why do I have these horrible thoughts/feelings about myself?"
Cure: Investigate your past.

The roots of low self-esteem run deep, and until you can uncover where they first began to grow, it can be hard to fully eradicate them. In fact, many people with low self-esteem don't realize that they are reenacting the messages and/or experiences they encountered in childhood.

As the clients I work with in my psychotherapy practice process their low self-esteem, they invariably realize that the particular kind of attention or love they desired in childhood was missing. Once you discover where these messages originated, you can stop letting them play on autopilot. Unlike when a kid is trapped in a bad situation, as an adult, you have a choice of how you deal with yourself—what messages you allow into your brain, with whom you choose to interact, and how kind you are in your interactions with yourself.

If you struggle with not feeling good enough on a chronic basis, it's almost 100 percent likely that something in your background has contributed to this. Examples include the obvious—physical or sexual abuse, which causes children or adolescents to feel an internalized sense of badness and self-blame for something that was done to them and that was never their fault. Medical illnesses, physical disabilities, and learning disabilities are a few other clear contributing factors to low self-esteem for some. There are also less overt examples that can contribute to low self-esteem. Even parents who are loving and attentive to their children can unknowingly set children up to feel poorly about themselves.

Self-Assessment: How Did Your Low Self-esteem Come to be?

Reflect on the following questions, and see if you can put together a picture of how it is you came to feel negatively about yourself.

- How did your family contribute to your self-esteem? Consider your relationships with your mother, father, and siblings—or anyone who was an immediate caregiver or family member.

- Did people say anything positive about you and if so, in what area(s) of your life? Consider if they were typically positive about your appearance, your schoolwork, your athletics, your friendships, your essence, or other activities. Alternatively, did no one remark about your positive qualities or help you to connect with positive aspect about yourself?

- What did your mother or father harp on or give you a hard time about? Write down the kinds of statements that you recall hearing on a recurrent basis that would make you feel badly. Notice character statements versus behavioral statements. Behavioral statements—"You need to be home by 11:00 p.m. on Friday nights, or you will not be able to use the car for the next week"—are benign, appropriate parenting techniques. Character statements—"You are always up to something, and you are a liar"—deplete self-worth.

- When you made mistakes or had setbacks how did your mother respond?

- When you made mistakes or had setbacks how did your father respond?

- Were you made to feel as if you were a "bad kid," or were your parents fairly balanced in their approach? A balanced approach is feeling loved and valued even when you mess up. "I love you, but you have to turn your homework in on time." A nonbalanced approach means you were made to feel like a failure or miserable person when you made mistakes. "You didn't turn in your homework, AGAIN! You're lazy! You're going to fail! Why can't you be more like Josh? He's making straight As!"

- When you fail or hit a setback or things don't go as you would like, do you tend to punish yourself in the same manner your parents did, or can you still show yourself unconditional love in the face of setbacks/mistakes?

- When you made a decision for yourself growing up (what college to go to, how to handle friendships and schoolwork, what to wear, how to wear your hair, how to dress, how to manage your free time) did your mother or father support your decisions or second guess and cause you to doubt yourself? Do you repeat this within yourself when you make decisions and does it contribute to your self-doubt/indecisiveness?

- When you expressed upset, disappointment, hurt, or generally a negative emotion, were you made to feel unsupported as a result, or could your parents validate your feelings? Feeling validated means they could muster something like "You're disappointed. I can understand how you would feel that way." Alternatively, if they were invalidating they might get angry and say, "I can't deal with this NOW!" or "You are too sensitive. Get over it."

- If your caregiver did not validate your feelings when you were young, do you repeat that approach when you experience disappointment? In other words, when you are upset, do you judge yourself for experiencing negative feelings—"What's wrong with me? I shouldn't feel this way," "I'm weak for crying," "I need to toughen up," "I'm too sensitive," or "I always feel bad. I'm a loser."

- When you had fun or enjoyed spontaneous activities in childhood or as a teenager, were you made to feel as if something bad was going to happen, that you did not deserve good experiences, or did you have a sense that you shouldn't have too much fun?

- Do you deal with having fun in the same manner now, so when you enjoy yourself you are afraid something bad is going to happen, feel guilty for having pleasure or perhaps not allow yourself to be spontaneous out of fear or guilt?

- Now consider your relationships with friends or peers while growing up. Did you have any periods of time where you felt left out or as if you did not have enough friends? What did you tell yourself about this? Could anyone help you make sense of it without blaming you or telling you what you were doing wrong to cause the situation?

- How did you perceive yourself as different from your peers while growing up—financially (was your family significantly different socioeconomically from most of your peers), family structure (divorce, gay parents, adoption, death or loss of a parent), medical issues, learning disabilities, parental health issues, parental psychological issues, sibling health or psychological issues—are examples.

- When friendships or romantic relationships aren't going well for you, do you feel the same way you felt when you were left out as a child?

- Did your peers ever bully you? How did you make sense of this, did you decide it was your fault?

- How did you do academically in school while growing up? Did you have a learning disability or anything that made schoolwork particularly challenging for you?

- If school was a struggle, how did you make sense of this struggle? In other words did you feel "stupid" or not as good as your peers? Did any adult in your life help you to understand this as something not inherently wrong or bad about you?

- If you struggled in school, do any of the same messages replay when you face adult achievement (work, school) setbacks?

This self-assessment may bring up some anger at your caregivers/teachers/peers, and it's okay to experience this. In fact it can be helpful to take some of the blame off yourself and recognize that perhaps you were not always treated fairly and kindly.

At the same time notice if you're in a perpetual blame and anger loop and try to go back to observing how you were treated and how this impacted the way you treat yourself now. Do you, now that you're an adult, use the same tone of voice or statements to beat yourself up as your parents or caregivers did when you were growing up?

Allow yourself to recognize what you needed from your caregivers/teachers/peers but did not receive. Let yourself understand what was missing, so you can stop repeating the past and start giving yourself what you always needed—unconditional love. Do that now. As you work on this, you will become much more likely to consciously develop friendships and romantic relationships with people who have the capacity to give you the love and respect that you deserve.

STEP 2

Connect With the Eye of Your Storm

For most of us, it's easy to feel as if our entire identity is merely a reflection of whatever we may be thinking or feeling in a particular moment. Like a distracted toddler, we get pulled in whatever direction our thoughts, emotions, or drives direct us. The feelings or thoughts that dominate our psyches moment by moment eventually evaporate and are replaced by new feelings and thoughts. Whatever the content of our minds in the moment, it generally tends to feel as if it represents a direct reflection of reality, who we are, and what we need to do.

Fact: You are not your emotions, your thoughts, or your urges. You are actually the one observing these experiences.

Like the eye of a hurricane, a calm center exists within you where you can observe passing storms, joy, pain and the flood of other emotions ever present in life *without becoming merged with them*. Even in flooding rain and gale-force wind, a calm center resides within you. Finding it means you are no longer the hurricane in your life; you observe it and are aware of it, but you no longer feel the hurricane represents who you are as a person.

Sit quietly somewhere, and allow your mind to drift. Notice where it is going—perhaps you recognize you are hungry and then start imagining what you would like for lunch. Lunch reminds you of a grocery list you need to write, and then you experience a sense of pressure to make time for the grocery store. Then anxiety seeps in as you realize you have another commitment tonight, so you will not be able to go to the store. Or perhaps you can somehow do both?

Alternatively, notice the physical sensations in your body. Perhaps your back is uncomfortable, or you have a headache. Search for the emotions you may be feeling. Is your chest tense? Are you anxious or sad?

As you observe your mind swirling, remind yourself that it is *you* observing your thoughts from the calm eye of the storm. If you observe over longer periods of time, you will notice that thoughts, emotions, and sensations tend to pass, only to get replaced by others. Yet the calm of the storm's eye never changes. You are not frightened by your thoughts because you know they are not you. You are the one observing them from a neutral place.

Your internal eye of calm is a stable place that is always there for you. It is where you find a conscious awareness of yourself in the world. As you become better connected with your eye—that which is observing all of the painful thoughts, emotions, and aches you experience—you will find comfort and safety. When you are in that place of calm, you are able to notice and acknowledge without becoming consumed.

Each time you encounter difficult feelings or painful thoughts about yourself, separate by becoming an observer. Notice what is happening as one emotion is replaced by another, like clouds changing in the sky.

Problem: "I don't know how to think differently about myself."
Cure: Label negative thinking patterns so you may unhook from them.

If you suffer from chronic low self-esteem, it's likely you are harboring certain schemas about yourself that are ineffective or toxic but reflect well-worn patterns of synaptic activity. You have a choice whether to allow a new, positive experience to take hold in your mind or to continue down the same old negative-thought streams. Engaging new patterns of positive-thought associations will change your neuronal circuitry and the way you feel about yourself.

Even when you feel defeated or disappointed, these *new ways of thinking about how you think* will cue up more easily so that you may engage with life more positively.

It's important to consider the content of your thoughts so they don't play out unchallenged. Consider what thought streams, memory sequences, or negative events tend to reappear in your mind.

As you begin to consciously observe your thought stream, notice how each thought influences the next. Perhaps you had a hard day at work or feel your boss doesn't value you, and then you flash back in time to an old flame who made you feel worthless, and you begin to remember the painful things the person said. As this thought spools out, you feel progressively worse. As you gain greater conscious awareness of your thoughts, it will be easier to pull out of negative-thought spirals and engage with the present moment. The more you understand how your thoughts work, the easier it will be to connect with your internal eye of calm.

Develop your awareness of problematic thinking spirals that make you feel poorly about yourself through *identifying your automatic thoughts, core beliefs,* and *errors in thinking.*

Automatic Thoughts

Thinking is a way for us to understand and interpret what is going on in the environment and in our interactions with others. Thoughts, some helpful and others less helpful, bombard our minds constantly.

Automatic thoughts are the instantaneous meanings and interpretations you give to your experiences. They pop into your head quickly, and most of the time you are not specifically aware of them. What people usually experience from these automatic thoughts is emotion and, in the case of some thoughts, heated emotion. By the time you recognize you're upset or anxious or sad, you may not recall the particular automatic thought that generated the negative emotion.

Everyone has automatic thoughts, and they are often distorted in some way, but yet we react as if they are a true reflection of reality and ourselves.

What you are *thinking* about yourself impacts how you are *feeling* about yourself. Inaccuracies and negative distortions in thought patterns lead to upsetting emotions. Identifying and challenging your automatic thoughts will help you to feel better.

Self-Assessment: Identify Your Automatic Thoughts.

Call to mind some occasions this week when you experienced a negative emotion—sadness, anxiety, anger, hurt, defeat, disappointment. Call the situation to mind with vivid awareness, as if it were happening all over again.

1. Label the *emotion* you felt.
2. Next write down *what is going through your mind*—the automatic thoughts or automatic images that come to mind—when you feel this way.
3. Is the automatic thought a distortion? Think of ways it might not be true.
4. What's the *worst-case scenario* if the thought turns out to be accurate?
5. How could you *healthfully cope* if the worst-case scenario occurred? How could you right the ship, make yourself feel better, or repair your relationships with others? Imagine yourself making the worst-case scenario better. Work to believe you could.
6. What is the *impact on you of believing the automatic thought*? How would you feel if you stopped believing the automatic thought to be true?
7. Now search for *the middle path*—notice if you are going to extremes, and see if there is a more balanced or realistic interpretation of what you experienced. What would you tell a friend if she were experiencing similar thoughts about herself?

Take the example of Mia, whose automatic thoughts are underlined.

Mia felt consumed with loneliness and sadness. All she wanted to do was hear her ex's voice. She worked up all her nerve and called him. Here is what happened in Mia's words: "He answered but sounded distant. He was quiet and didn't say much on the phone. I was thinking he doesn't really care about me. I'm a burden to him now. He wants nothing to do with me. When we hung up, I felt like a repeat loser and sadder than before—I felt awful about myself, as if I were being rejected all over again."

Mia's automatic thoughts are generating her negative feelings about herself. These thoughts may be slightly distorted—he must care somewhat, or why would he take her call? One phone call is hardly a burden. If he wanted nothing to do with her, he likely would have been angrier or aggressively told her to never contact him again. On the other hand, perhaps it's true he really didn't feel comfortable talking with Mia because they are broken up.

So instead of interpreting the difficult conversation to mean that she was a miserable loser, an adaptive reframe for her to consider might be something such as this: "That was a really awkward and hard conversation. I was lonely and wanted to see if it would make me feel better to reach out to him, but it did not. Now I know that won't help. His distance is because we can't be close and are no longer in an intimate relationship. I need to work toward accepting this."

This week, when you notice your mood changing or that you are feeling poorly about yourself, stop and ask, "What was I just thinking about?" Work to no longer accept as true every automatic thought about yourself that goes through your head. Consider that some of these thoughts are inaccurate. They may be more related to your belief that you are not good enough as opposed to actually not being good enough in reality. Notice if certain situations or people evoke similar automatic thoughts.

Core Beliefs

Now that you are becoming open to the idea that some of your thoughts are inaccurate or distorted, examine your core beliefs. In cognitive therapy, core beliefs represent our most central ideas about who we are. You may generally have core beliefs that are positive about yourself: "I can do most things well," "I am likable," "I'm a competent person," or "Most of my close friends love me." In times of stress, however, negative core beliefs tend to surface.

Negative core beliefs are overgeneralized and rigid, global ideas about yourself. When a core belief is activated, you can probably only think of information that supports it, and it becomes difficult to think about yourself in a more realistic or balanced way. Negative core beliefs tend to develop in childhood and may become powerfully reinforced when similar situations call them up. When unchallenged, repeated exposure to these negative thoughts makes them seem more and more accurate. However, just like automatic thoughts, core beliefs can be evaluated and modified.

Negative core beliefs typically fall into two general categories: beliefs associated with helplessness and beliefs associated with unlovability.

Examples of Helpless Core Beliefs:

- I'm inadequate.
- I'm a failure.
- I'm not good enough.
- I'm helpless.
- I'm powerless.
- I'm weak.

Examples of Unlovable Core Beliefs:

- I'm unworthy.
- I'm unlovable.
- I'm bad.
- I'm unlikeable.
- I'm unwanted.
- I'm not good enough.

Go back to the internal-critic exercise in step one, where you considered the themes of your internal dialogue and wrote some examples down in your notebook. As you review these themes, does your internal critic tend to be more likely to tell you that you are unlovable or that you are helpless as a person? Ask yourself what the voice in your head is telling you about who you are at your core. Is it telling you that you are an inadequate person or a person whom no one could love?

Exercise: Uncover Your Core Beliefs

Complete the following sentences to understand what fear is at the bottom of your upset and distorted view about yourself:

- If I am not loved by everyone, then…
- If I am not perfectly competent, then…
- If there is the possibility of me making a mistake, then…

- If I am afraid/anxious, then…
- If I don't work hard, then…
- If I work really hard, then…
- If I am happy, then…
- If people criticize me, then…
- If people leave me out, then…
- If people reject me, then…
- I won't be happy unless…

The sentences above should help you to generate what you are afraid will happen to you in your mind's worst-case scenario. These fears likely represent your negative core beliefs about yourself. As you review the fears you have written down, ask yourself this question: is your vulnerability centered around fears of failure and lack of achievement, or is your vulnerability more a fear of being left out and unloved?

Exercise: Challenge Your Core Beliefs

To challenge your negative core beliefs about yourself, keep in mind the following things:

- Even though your negative core beliefs feel very real and true to you, they are still mostly—or even completely—untrue.

- Core beliefs usually are the result of childhood events, parental treatment, or culture, and they may not have been true even at the time you first came to believe them.

- What makes core beliefs seem so true is that every time you encounter certain data that supports that core belief, you pay attention to it and disregard data to the contrary.

- You can change these ideas about yourself and view yourself in a more realistic way.

Try to work toward developing a more adaptive core belief about your deepest self. It doesn't have to be an unrealistically positive perspective. It should take into account both what you struggle with and also your strengths.

Actively look for evidence and examples that might contradict your core belief, or try to see if you can come up with a way to adaptively reframe your perspective.

Old core belief: "I'm weak and ineffective."
New belief: "I have control over many things."

Old core belief: "I'm unlovable."
New core belief: "I'm generally someone people like."

Old core belief: "I'm permanently flawed."
New core belief: "I'm normal and have strengths and weaknesses."

Self-Talk

If you struggle with low self-esteem, then you likely continually talk to yourself in a biased manner about yourself and your experiences. To develop a more supportive way of talking to yourself, you need to be able to identify when the voice in your head is distorting the facts and causing you undue upset.

"Errors in Thinking" List:

There are a number of common distortions in thinking that people typically make, and these distortions intensify negative feelings. If you familiarize yourself with these errors in thinking, then it will be easier to talk yourself out of the negative feelings you are experiencing.

- **Black-and-White Thinking:** Things are all good or all bad; you are perfect or a failure. Are you considering the nuance and complexity of people, interactions, and events, or are you only looking at things from polarized perspectives?

- **Overgeneralization:** This is taking one event or scenario to mean a pervasive pattern of failure or defeat. If something negative happens in one context, it means it will continue to happen. "I was awkward and boring on that date. I don't have what it takes to have a comfortable romantic relationship."

- **Seeing Catastrophe:** You look into the future with sweeping negativity instead of a more balanced perspective. "I had an argument with my significant other. We are always going to be unhappy."

- **Emotional Reasoning:** You think something is true and accurate because you feel it so intensely and ignore contradictory evidence. "I feel as if he doesn't care about me, so that means he doesn't care about me." You assume your emotions reflect the way things truly are. "I feel unattractive and boring, so I must be unattractive and boring."

- **Filtering:** You focus on a negative detail and filter out the positive details. Hyperfocusing on a negative magnifies it and distorts the bigger picture. "I got a C on that test. Even though the rest of my test grades are higher, I'm not doing at all well in this class."

- **Personalization:** This is believing that how others treat you is always a direct and personal reflection of how they feel about you. You fail to consider other more reasonable explanations. "My mother-in-law is ignoring me because I did something wrong."

- **Labeling:** This is applying a fixed, global label to yourself or others without including any context. This labeling increases the negative emotion and intensity associated with the situation. "I'm a loser." "He's a jerk." "I'm fat." "She's a slut." "He's a player."

- **Should-ing and Must-ing:** You have rigid expectations for how you or others should act, and when these expectations aren't met, you overemphasize the negative consequences. "I *shouldn't* have called her. I'm such a loser." "I *should* exercise. I'm so lazy." The consequences of such statements are guilt when directed toward yourself or frustration when directed toward others.

- **Mind Reading:** This is believing others know what you are thinking or that you know what they are thinking. You fail to communicate directly about what you are thinking or consider other possibilities for what others may have on their minds. "She's thinking I'm boring and uninteresting," or "He's got to know I want him to call me."

- **Demonizing or Idealizing:** You see others in your life (and yourself) as perfect until they disappoint you, and then you see them as the enemy. "He's perfect. I'm so lucky. We never fight, and he's the best person in the world" morphs into "He's a sociopath with no conscience."

The next exercise will help you identify errors in thinking and cut off negative-thinking spirals before they make you feel unworthy and ineffective.

Exercise: Take a Thought Inventory

When you notice you are upset or feeling negative about yourself, pull out this thought inventory so that you can better connect with your internal eye. The more you use this inventory, the quicker new ways of thinking will become automatic and easy to access.

- What was the event, situation, thought, mental image, or memory that you remember encountering before your feelings shifted?

- Label how you feel—angry, sad, anxious, upset, ashamed, guilty, hopeless—and label how intense those feelings are. (Use a scale of zero to ten to rate the intensity.)

- What physical sensations do you notice in your body? What do you want to do? What actions did you take (if any)?

- What automatic thoughts were running through your head after or during the event? Ask yourself, "What was I thinking?" or "What was running through my mind at the time?" Write down the thoughts that brought you the most distress and how much you believe these thoughts. (Use a scale of zero to ten.)

- What core beliefs are underpinning these automatic thoughts? Ask yourself, if these automatic thoughts are true, what does it mean about you as a person? If, for instance, you think that you will never be worthy of love or that you are a defective human being, what will be the result? Write these beliefs down and rate how much you believe them. (Use a scale of zero to ten.)

- Can you identify any distortions in your thinking? Look back at the self-talk section above for examples. Write about how you may be distorting your thinking here—that is, seeing catastrophe, black-and-white thinking, mind reading, emotional reasoning.

- Write down evidence supporting these negative thoughts about yourself.

- Write down evidence or examples disproving these same negative thoughts about yourself.

- Now write down a more realistic interpretation of the events—not overly inflated or positive, just what a reasonable person might think. Consider other ways to interpret the situation or what you might say to a friend who was thinking these same thoughts.

Summary

There is a difference between feeling bad and being a bad person, feeling sad and becoming a depressed person, doubting yourself and becoming down and negative, feeling angry and punching someone. The difference is getting in touch with the part of you that can observe your thoughts and sensations without allowing yourself to become what you feel.

No matter what the weather is like in your life at any particular moment, becoming aware of your thought patterns and challenging your irrational thinking will enable you to be more comfortable with yourself.

Like sitting in a protected alcove while observing a hurricane around you, your internal eye is safe and does not bring pain. Your eye is wise and knows that whatever urgent need, painful emotion, or upsetting thought you are experiencing in this moment will pass. Just as the clouds move through the sky, thoughts and feelings come and go. Change is constant, and accepting this fact brings peace.

STEP 3

Radically Accept

One of the most difficult of human conditions is a sense of not feeling quite good enough. Believing you are somehow missing the mark means you spin your wheels with anxious energy by constantly weighing out how to get it "right," how to appear "good enough," and ways to dupe people into thinking you are better than you believe yourself to be. And a lack of self-acceptance and chronically feeling inherently wrong are made exponentially worse when we face difficult life events. If you are going through a divorce or break up, or you're having difficulty with work or with the people you love in your life, then you may judge yourself more harshly than ever.

Feeling as if something fundamental is missing from your core means you don't see yourself as belonging to the larger whole, and this brings on a crushing sense of aloneness. The lack of self-acceptance means you project onto others your disharmonious sense of self, and you are less likely to feel at ease with the people in your life. You may perceive that life is constantly hard.

You have the capacity to change this. Radical self-acceptance is the key to internal peace no matter what obstacles you face.

Feeling not good enough may have become such a robust mental habit that the neurons in your brain have acquired a hair trigger when it comes to recalling negative stories about yourself.

One result of unrelenting self-criticism is a desperate need to feel better. In this situation, a person may turn anywhere in hopes of relief—unhealthy new relationships, an extraordinary effort to never be alone, sex without desire, compulsive achievement, constant attention to busyness, plastic surgery, dieting, material possessions—the list is long.

But at the same time, there persists a lingering and well-founded sense that these tactics will never really cure the problem because, after all, you can't really escape yourself. The hopelessness that this engenders may lead to seeking relief through destructive behaviors—drug abuse, alcoholism, binge eating, not eating, shopping addiction, sexual addiction, hyperconsumerism—anything to feel better...if only briefly.

All human beings struggle with imperfection, and all human beings suffer; it's a component of human existence. Accepting this reality means when you are suffering, you can just suffer, as opposed to also berating yourself for something that is a natural part of the human condition.

Habitually critical ways of interacting with yourself can be changed. If you are reading this book you, along with most of humanity, struggle with self-acceptance. The first step in changing your mental wiring is to recognize how you have chosen to cope with this deficit. Come to terms with the behaviors you use (your "drug of choice") for medicating your self-esteem deficit, and recognize if you sponge off of others in a desperate quest to feel worthy.

Destructive Ways of Coping

For Jenna, it took all of her mental energy to simply get through the day and do what was required of her. She went through her work life with a stiff upper lip. As a professionally successful sales associate, she always put on a happy face and enthusiastic attitude. Even when sales fell, she would inspire her team, cheering them on to do better. She had a reputation around the office of someone who never let anything get her down. When she saw friends or family, she did not share much about herself but was ready to support them. However, Jenna crumbled when she was alone. Her friends, family, and work associates would never have recognized the alone Jenna. It was the complete opposite of the public Jenna. She was deeply unhappy, aimless, and confused about what to do or how to deal with herself. Jenna so detested being alone that she worked herself to the bone all day and into the evening. She would prefer to see a friend on the way home from work or work until 11:00 p.m.—anything to avoid being alone with herself in her apartment.

When she did finally go home, she would numb her emotions by bingeing on junk food and zoning out watching TV until the wee hours of the morning. The only way she nurtured herself was with food. The morning after a binge, Jenna would harshly scold herself—"Stop binge eating or else!"—and then repeat the pattern that evening.

If you struggle with low self-esteem, you may feel as if you're perpetually grinding your gears to get through the day. Addiction may beckon as a way to glide free for a short period of time—alcohol, drugs, sex, compulsive dating, the Internet, pornography, compulsive shopping. With so little self-nurturing, you search for a way to disconnect from yourself and from the world around you.

Take a clear look at the destructive ways you cope with not feeling good enough. This analysis will help you come to terms with how much you need real care and nurturance.

Do You Sponge Off Others for Your Self-Worth?

If you struggle with chronic low self-esteem, then you are susceptible to looking for quick fixes to feel a modicum of value or worth. One particularly prevalent way to feel special and worthy is through the attention of others. The flip side of this is something I call *the sponge effect*. This comes when you are so desperate for the validation and approval of others that you become highly vulnerable to their negative emotions and reactions. You may soak up the negative emotions of others or take on excess responsibility to please and keep others happy.

Also if you compulsively depend on others to validate your worth, then you may be susceptible to blaming yourself for the negative things that occur in your life—romantic rejection, work setbacks, or issues with friends—and fail to consider other more likely explanations.

You do not have a separate sense of self if your self-worth depends on how others are treating you and on what accolades you are receiving professionally or socially.

Recognize if you consistently farm out your worth to others. Notice how this makes you vulnerable because the whims and opinions of others are fickle and unsteady. Stop tuning into how others are interacting with you, and tune into what's going on for you now, in your own body. See how you experience yourself through your own eyes. What do you like, dislike, and need?

Instead of imagining what someone else might think of you, redirect your attention to your thoughts about what *you need* to be fully healthy. Observe when you feel a sense of internal peace, even if it's fleeting, or when you feel displeasure. If you are ambivalent, rather than just going forth or asking others their opinions, sit down and try to work through the ambivalence.

Now let's turn to the work of helping you to connect with your worth separate from others.

Problem: "I don't know a better way."
Cure: Start a new relationship with yourself.

Too often people beat themselves up for not handling a particular relationship adequately, for causing distress to another, or for not doing enough for someone else. In my experience, this kind of self-criticism means people try harder for a bit, only to fall back into the same problematic patterns. In reality, what helps individuals to be truly understanding of others is the capacity to be deeply compassionate with themselves.

Women in particular are socialized to tune into the feelings of others more than their own feelings. For some, it becomes a compulsion to make sure everyone else is okay before actually attending to how they themselves are feeling. This results in lopsided relationships where the woman involved is so consumed by taking care of the needs of her partners, children, parents, and friends that she may not even recognize how out of touch she is with her own needs.

Self-compassion means self-acceptance, faults and all. And it means recognizing that the experience of life is connected to the larger collective human experience.

Whatever you are struggling with in your head about yourself, allow it to be present with self-compassion and not self-criticism. When you unreservedly accept yourself, you will feel truly free and at ease; this leads to more intimacy with others, which provides a resilient buffer to all that ails you.

Being intimate with yourself means you accept yourself just as you are. Even when your emotions, actions, and reactions are painful, frustrating, or embarrassing, you hold onto these experiences with loving kindness.

Becoming more intimate with yourself in this way will have a far-reaching impact, improving the quality of your romantic relationships and friendships, as well as enhancing your motivation and drive to get what you want out of life. Acceptance doesn't mean you do not want to change some aspects of yourself. In fact, acceptance makes growth possible.

Humanizing Your Internal Critic

For many, an internal critic is always present and, at the same time, intangible. Carrying around this sense that "I'm not doing enough" or "Something is inherently flawed about me" means you can never quite be yourself with others.

For example, when Anya became more in touch with her internal narrative, she realized that every time there was a lull or pause in her day-to-day activity, her internal voice was telling her, "You're fat. You're so disgusting, no one wants you." Anya wouldn't allow herself to go to the gym out of fear that others would see her weight, pity her, and think, "Why is she working out? What's the sense?" She labored compulsively to avoid herself. Anya had no intimate relationships because she was terrified people would see all she hated about herself. At the same time, she was afraid to be alone because that was when her internal critic attacked her. To compensate, when she found herself alone, she'd numb out with self-destructive behaviors.

Anya worked in therapy on becoming more aware of how she interacted with herself. She started to notice that her internal voice was consistently mean and punitive. She eventually drew a connection between the voice in her head and her mother, who was critical and dissatisfied with Anya throughout her childhood. She came to see how she picked up where her mother left off, mistreating and emotionally abusing herself in a similar manner. At first, she had difficulty softening the voice in her head. Eventually Anya was able to conjure up the voice of her father, who had passed away years earlier. Each time she recognized her suffering, she imagined him saying, "You are worth it. You are strong and capable. I'm proud of you." These three sentences and imagining herself through her father's eyes began a process that inspired new thoughts about herself and allowed her to have new experiences.

Anya's consistency with this approach changed the way she interacted with herself. She became more accepting. She began to finally enjoy being alone. She said it became the one time of the day "that I have no pressure from anyone to be a certain way or to take care of others. I'm free to just be me."

It's by looking your experience straight in the eye—through reflection and self-observation—that negative elements lose their power. You no longer have to live in fear of your internal experience and search for quick fixes or ways to camouflage, mask, or distract. Memories of negative experiences are no longer bad and scary. They can be present, and you can sit with them and reflect.

Now if all you do is reflect, you may become self-critical again, so while reflecting, take a compassionate stance with yourself.

Here are three ways to be more compassionate as you privately reflect:

1. Remind yourself that all human beings struggle with negative aspects of existence. There is nothing wrong with you or bad about you because you too struggle and suffer.
2. Use a kind tone. Be soft with yourself. If you can't find this tone, try to imagine someone who loves you talking to you and supporting you— a parent, friend, sibling, grandparent, teacher, coach, old lover, deceased relative. Imagine that person seeing only good in you. How would that person talk to you about your struggles?
3. As you notice your feelings, reactions, or physical sensations—say to yourself, "This feeling can be here as long as it needs to be," "I can embrace this thing that I so hate about myself," "I'm a soft container that can hold all that I struggle with," and "I can comfort myself while taking note of my suffering."

Exercise: Stop and Reflect

Sit quietly and comfortably and listen to your internal narrative. Notice if the voice in your head speaks to you in a judgmental or angry tone and how this tends to add to your insecurities and tension. Consider softening the tone and making it more supportive of you and your goals.

Label whatever is going on in your physical body without judgment—heart beating fast…muscles tight…head heavy…sickness in stomach…chest tight. There is no right or wrong. Just observe and label.

As you sit quietly, consider the physical, emotional, mental, and acting parts of yourself.

Can you accept your *physical self* (aches, pains, health, feeling physically unhealthy, medication needs), your *emotional self* (low moods, anxious moments, emotional ups and downs, jealous feelings, shame, guilt, anger, frustration), your *mental self* (intellectual capacity, dark thoughts, mental limitations, aggressive thoughts) and your *acting self* (acting mean or petty toward others, not following through on commitments, not doing what you think you should be doing, procrastination)—can you *compassionately accept* all of these parts of you, just as they are right now in this moment?

When you notice frustration building, an urgent need to take a particular action, the onset of anxiety or sadness, instead of instantly distracting yourself with social media, the Internet, busyness, or warm bodies, sit with your experience. Gently label it, and sit with it by telling yourself, "This feeling can be here as long as it needs to be," "It doesn't mean anything bad about me that I'm experiencing this right now," and "Thoughts and feelings come and go. I'm going to stay present with this one while it's here." As you become closer with your experience, you become intimate and connected with yourself.

Each time you do this exercise, you are working toward embracing yourself fully. You are showing yourself that you can be present with every wonderful and difficult thing about you, and you will see that nothing bad will happen.

Becoming Your Own Best Caretaker

Imagine your relationship with yourself—how you talk, interact, support, and punish yourself—as being similar to how you would treat a small child entrusted to your care. If the child told you she had a hard day, would you berate the child and remind her of her every imperfection or past mistake? As she enjoys friends or completes her homework, would you pull her attention away and remind her of how she blew it with her last best friend or did poorly on a recent school exam? Would you allow the child to stay up all night and eat junk food, day after day? Would you encourage a child in your care to starve herself to lose weight? Would you use a harsh and abusive tone toward the child?

When those with low self-esteem consider these questions, they report that they would take better care of a child than they do of themselves. Children benefit from a daily routine that includes a safe and relaxing environment with an emotionally supportive and positive parent, some physical exercise, stimulating activities, and warm kindness—adults who treat themselves with this same magic recipe tend to feel better about themselves.

Another component in developing a new relationship with yourself, in addition to humanizing your internal critic, is learning to become your own best caretaker by developing what I call "daily rituals of self-love." People who generally feel positively about themselves tend to do these things automatically.

Exercise: Develop Daily Rituals of Self-love

Consciously work to adopt these healthy routines, and they will eventually become a natural part of your day.

- **Stress-Reducing Ritual:** Engage in a relaxation activity for at least ten minutes every day. This could take many forms—for example, meditation, breathing exercises, mindfulness, or yoga.

- **Beginning and End-of-Day Rituals:** Give yourself a brief beginning-of-day ritual in which you muster your energy for what is ahead, and create an end-of-day ritual in which you praise yourself for the effort you have made, regardless of whether you've been successful or not.

- **Healthy-Eating Ritual:** You do not need to be a perfect eater, but do consider adding healthy foods to your daily diet.

- **Positive-Others Rituals:** Work most days to engage at least one person who believes in you and sees you more positively than you see yourself.

- **Intellectual-Stimulation Ritual:** Work each day to grow your brain. Read books, newspapers, listen to NPR, write about your self-growth, read this workbook, take a class, learn to knit, complete home-repair projects, tinker with new electronic devices. Give your brain a meaningful activity so it won't use excess energy to attack your self-esteem.

- **Exercise Ritual:** Participate in moderate exercise most days of the week.

- **General Life-Upkeep Ritual:** Spend some time most days on the paperwork or the administrative/business aspects of your life. Alternate between such tasks as paying bills, budgeting, cleaning your living space, grocery shopping, errands, and laundry.

Stress is greatly reduced when we develop behavioral habits and rituals that lessen anxiety. Neuronal growth occurs when we learn new information, but new growth actually decreases when we are in a stressed-out state of mind. The hippocampus (the brain's memory storehouse) is dependent on glucose for energy. Stress hormones decrease glucose in the brain and render the hippocampus less effective. If you undertake the exercises in this workbook while experiencing anxiety, worry, or repetitive negative thoughts, the new learning will not be as effectively imprinted in your memory. This is why the daily rituals are important. *Each day, no matter what you experience in your environment or in your head, search for a measure of peace.*

If you start your day already feeling behind, then you are going to experience any curveball that comes your way as defeat. This leads to feeling as if you are somehow doomed to never get what you need or want out of life because of your inherent flaws.

Start the day with a morning routine that helps you feel grounded and in control. People vary widely on this—for one person it may be a shower, getting dressed, drinking tea, and reading the news. For another, it may mean coffee and ten minutes of silence before he is ready to plug in. And still another may start with a vigorous walk or workout. The point is to reflect on what brings you peace and well-being as you start your day. Then make it happen, and hold yourself accountable for its recurrence.

Healthy nutrition, exercise, intellectual stimulation, positive people, and overall life upkeep are key ingredients to feeling good enough. You don't have to be perfect, but try to get a little of all of these in, perhaps not every day, but most days of the week. Operating in this way means you're not constantly dreading what you have been avoiding or beating yourself up about all you still have to do.

Imagine life as akin to water in a cup: if your cup is too full, there is no space to take on any more stress or effectively manage life's ups and downs. If you generally participate in these rituals of self-love, then the water in your cup will decrease. This allows room for you to cope with the negative life events and emotional experiences that are inevitable.

Life is hard enough. Knowing you have your house in order puts a buffer between you and the world's many trials.

STEP 4

Change Your Approach To Setbacks

O ne sure way to avoid failure is by never taking on anything you are not absolutely positive will be a success. In terms of reaching your professional, academic, social, and relationship goals, this is a tactic that will hold you back. Of course, taking on challenges that you may not be able to meet means risking setbacks. But you will spin your wheels and make little forward progress as long as you see setbacks as failures.

Carol Dweck, professor and leading researcher in the area of social and developmental psychology, developed a theory of success that is based upon extensive laboratory research. According to Dweck, people tend to develop a *mindset*, which is an internalized belief about what fosters their successes and failures. There are two kinds of mindset—fixed and growth. A fixed mindset is characterized by believing that we are born with a preordained amount of "stuff," whether that stuff is intelligence, personality, mood, athleticism, humor—and we either have these natural abilities or we do not. A fixed mindset is an all-or-nothing way of thinking about yourself—"Either I am a loser or a success," "Either I am a good person or a bad person," or "Either I am desirable or undesirable."

Dweck found that praising children with labels—for example, making statements such as "you are so smart"—actually creates a fixed mindset and lowers IQ scores. Using all-or-nothing labels, such as "smart," "athletic," "brilliant," or "beautiful," indirectly communicates to children that nothing will ever be a challenge because their innate abilities protect them. When they inevitably face difficulty or setbacks, self-esteem collapses, and fixed-mindset individuals tend to give up.

On the other hand, a growth mindset acknowledges that we are born with certain temperamental and genetic propensities but experience and learning are what cause people to grow. While fixed-mindset individuals believe having to work at something means they are not smart/good enough, growth-mindset individuals believe effort and hard work pay off. When faced with negative feedback or when a flaw is exposed, growth-mindset individuals work harder and become more curious about finding an effective strategy.

Here are statements from Carol Dweck's *Mindset: The New Psychology of Success*[1] with which *fixed-mindset* individuals agree.

- "You are a certain kind of person, and there is not much that can be done to really change that."
- "You can do things differently, but the important parts of who you are can't really be changed."

Here are statements with which *growth-mindset* individuals agree.

- "No matter what kind of a person you are, you can always change substantially."
- "You can always change basic things about the kind of person you are."

Fixed-mindset individuals feel shame and tend to give up when their shortcomings are exposed; for them, shortcomings mean they have permanent flaws that cannot ever be improved. As a result, fixed-mindset individuals work hard to cover up their flaws. They are hypersensitive to perceived criticism and meet failures with defensiveness. For the fixed-mindset individual, self-esteem is entirely dependent upon being right and perfect. They prove their worth by taking on low-risk experiences and relationships that do not challenge them. When failure occurs, fixed-mindset individuals tend to fall apart. They face a flood of

---

1 C. S. Dweck, *Mindset: The New Psychology of Success*, (Random House: New York, 2006).

negative emotion that leaves no room to strategize or otherwise mitigate their circumstances.

Failure is painful for growth-mindset individuals too, but they tend to look at their setbacks as opportunities to learn and grow. Each relationship that does not work out and each goal that goes unreached are experienced as ways to gain useful feedback and develop as a person. This point of view helps maintain self-esteem, even in the face of heartbreak and adversity.

Dweck researched individuals with depression and looked at their mindsets. She found both fixed- and growth-mindset individuals get depressed. As growth-mindset individuals became more depressed, they actually took on greater responsibility to manage their problems. They compensated by working harder to take care of themselves and to keep up with their lives.

What Is Your Approach to Setbacks?

Take the example of Carrie, who grew up aware that she was academically gifted. Throughout her school years, she was endlessly told she was smart, gifted, and naturally talented. She breezed through school and never hit a roadblock...until college. Once she became deeply entrenched in her engineering major, academics became extremely challenging, and making straight As became an impossible goal. Carrie's self-esteem plummeted. For the first time in her life, Carrie told herself she was not smart. In fact, she decided, she was a loser and was not cut out for an engineering degree. Carrie would not allow herself to ask for help—for her, this would be a public admission of stupidity and would bring unbearable shame.

She eventually gave up engineering altogether and took on a less challenging undergraduate major. Even after college, as a thirty-year-old, Carrie is still afraid to admit to friends and family when she is having a hard time emotionally or to ask for help on any matter. She remains committed to the belief that she is not good enough. Frightened that she will be exposed as a fraud, she does not seek opportunities for full-time work, and her naturally intellectual brain is stifled. She is bored and unfulfilled by her life.

Carrie is an example of what happens when a person's identity becomes entirely wrapped up in being the "smart one." This also occurs when a person's identity is centered on being the "pretty one," the "athletic one," the "womanizing one," or the "fun one." At some point, the person gets evidence that contradicts this fixed identity, and suddenly he stops believing in himself. He gives up pursuing his goals and actualizing his true potential.

Ask yourself this: Do you believe you are worthwhile even when you are not meeting the expectations of others? Or do feelings of worthlessness take over when you receive criticism? Does a bad day make you feel as if you are a deficient person? If so, you are disconnected from an internal sense of fulfillment and only value yourself when others do. This means you may shy away from challenges, taking on new projects, and actualizing your goals because of a fear that you will not be successful and will be exposed as inadequate, not attractive enough, not good enough, not smart enough.

The truth is, you're right. You won't immediately be successful in reaching your goals and meeting your challenges. Most people are not. Those who are successful work at it over a long period of time, and they do it by accepting criticism and feedback as specific ways to grow and improve.

If you take negative feedback as a black-and-white judgment about your worth, then you will give up each time you face adversity. No one gets what she wants without dealing with stumbling blocks. What's important is how you view and manage criticism and setbacks, which are part and parcel of pursuing any worthwhile goal.

Self-Assessment: Determine Your Life Approach.[2]

Take this self-assessment to find out if you allow yourself to grow from your mistakes, or if your mistakes signify to you that you are impossibly flawed. More yeses suggest you are prone toward not allowing yourself to evolve to become the person you wish to be. If you continually gauge your worth by how others see you, your self-esteem will remain fragile.

- When I hit a setback, I doubt myself and often give up.

- When something doesn't work out for me, I beat myself up with criticism.

2 Based on Carol Dweck's "mindset" theory. See C. S. Dweck, *Self-Theories: Their Role in Motivation, Personality, and Development,* (Psychology Press: New York and London, 2000). Also see C. S. Dweck, *Mindset: The New Psychology of Success,* (Random House: New York, 2006).

- Even when I do achieve a goal, I immediately begin to feel anxious about the next task on my list.

- Most of what I do is to prove my worth to others. It's not so much about what I desire.

- When I sense that someone is about to give me negative feedback, I withdraw, change the subject, or become defensive.

- I do not believe that I can grow from my mistakes.

- I want to stay just as I am, but I am unhappy where I am.

- Sometimes after a social event I feel great about myself, but then within a few hours or a day, I feel depleted.

- I am always worried that people will see me as a fraud, and I will be exposed.

- I do not believe that the aspects of my personality that bother me are changeable through learning and new experience.

Do You See Yourself At The Mercy of Circumstance?

If you grew up with parents who continually emphasized effort and personal responsibility, you may have an easier time with life's ups and downs. On the other hand, if your parental models continually blamed external factors for their difficulties, or if you genuinely struggled with events outside of your control (socioeconomic status, chronic childhood bullying, emotional trauma, physical abuse, neglect, war, or social unrest), you may be prone to feeling you are at the mercy of chance or circumstance.

The belief that your grit, persistence, and hard work will pay off is associated with a range of positive well-being variables including prohealth behaviors, emotional stability, relationship satisfaction, and professional accomplishment. The belief that they are not in control and they cannot right their own ships makes people more prone to depression and other serious problems, but this propensity can be overcome.

Self-Assessment: What is Your Attributional Style?

It is important for your future contentment to consider your perception of how much control you have over getting what you want out of life. Answer these questions to find out.

- Do you believe positive events in your life are mainly due to luck or chance?

- When you hit a setback or fail at something, do you blame others?

- When you are upset, do you feel as if your emotions are out of your control?

- When you have an argument with a friend or romantic partner, do you repeatedly tell yourself what the other person did wrong?

- When you hit a roadblock or challenge (interpersonally or professionally), do you tend to give up—that is, do you want to break up or switch job assignments?

Answering "yes" to all of these questions suggests you don't see your own potential for control/power in your life. Answering "yes" to a few suggests you externalize in some situations. Identifying specific factors that you can control when you experience setbacks will have a significant impact on your self-perception and your ability to get what you want in life. Self-determination is a remedy for feeling perpetually and passively victimized.

Problem: "When I make mistakes or receive negative feedback, it means I'm flawed as a person, forever doomed to not get what I want out of life."
Cure: Change your approach to setbacks.

If you have a high external locus of control or a fixed mindset, you may continually find yourself experiencing the same set of negative consequences; this may occur interpersonally, professionally, emotionally, and even in terms of your physical health.

If your philosophy holds that control is outside of your zone of influence, then you are essentially a slave to life, repeating the same negative dynamics again and again, all the while feeling at the mercy of circumstance. If it is common for you to face failure by giving up while also dwelling on all your other various shortcomings, you are boxing yourself off from ever feeling good enough. Over time, reenacting the same problematic patterns of behavior causes a self-fulfilling prophecy to manifest.

Whenever you find yourself upset or stuck over a relationship, work event, or family occurrence, notice if you are feeling like you are at the mercy of others or blaming them for your hardships or negative feelings. Even if your blame is warranted, wallowing in it is not going to help you to achieve your goals or make you feel any better. Instead, improve the way you treat yourself when hardship and disappointment come.

Here are a few strategies to help you to start seeing yourself as a work in progress as opposed to a success or failure.

- **You Are Your Own Most Potent Ally:** If you become harsh and self-critical when faced with your shortcomings, you are turning on the one person who can do the most to help. And too, relentless critical thinking writes the script for a self-fulfilling prophecy of failure. It is a very powerful act to rewrite the script, drop gloomy resignation, and resolve to work toward greater self-determination. Do not globally condemn yourself. List specific weaknesses you have (fear of commitment, procrastination, chronic tardiness, or fear of change), but also list ways to challenge yourself to mitigate these weaknesses and grow.

- **Cultivate Goals Based on Personal Desires:** When you feel as if your successes and failures are a statement of your worth, challenges are particularly intimidating because too much of your self-worth is at stake. On the other hand, self-esteem skyrockets when you cultivate goals based upon your innermost desires and when you develop a belief that persistence will enable you to realize these goals.

- **Train The Voice In Your Head To Be Kind:** When you experience failure or receive negative feedback, notice what your internal narrative tells you about the setback. Is there kindness in your internal voice, or is it a punitive voice? Notice the tone—is it harsh and angry or soft and compassionate? Let the voice kindly remind you that if you use the negative feedback to change, then you will grow and achieve.

- **Effort Pays Off:** Just as test scores are improved by studying, so too can self-esteem scores be improved with practice. Remind yourself effort pays off, and notice when you are punishing yourself for a perceived defect. Find a way to see yourself as a work in progress. When you want to give up in your pursuit of feeling better about yourself, persevere despite doubts or second thoughts.

- **Push Yourself:** You are strengthening your brain each time you challenge yourself with experiences that do not come easily. Intentionally seek experiences that are hard for you so you may learn to become more at ease with uncertainty. Surround yourself with people who challenge you intellectually, romantically, and emotionally.

- **Take On New Professional And Social Ventures:** Even when new activities and initiatives make you feel uncomfortable, do them anyway so that you will push yourself to find strategies for managing. If you struggle with communicating your needs or handling conflict in relationships with romantic partners, keep in mind that each relationship is an opportunity to work on improving these specific skills. Stop avoiding what scares you or makes you doubt yourself. Build a positive self-experience by showing you can confront what does not come easily.

Exercise: Radically Accept

Effort, hard work, learning from setbacks, soliciting feedback—these are the ingredients for reaching your goals successfully. If you are doing well at something, it is not necessarily because you are naturally gifted. Sure, that doesn't hurt, but it's much more likely that you're doing well because you persevere in spite of missteps, self-doubt, and criticism. Your actions (or inaction) are the most compelling force driving you to achieve what you want out of life.

Spend a few moments recalling the last time you heard criticism or received negative feedback from another person—or a bad grade, a job loss, a demotion, or a negative work review.

Now write down what your internal critic is/was telling you about the meaning of this negative feedback.

Next, work to accept without equivocation that you must change something as a result of the feedback, something specific.

For example, imagine your internal critic is saying, "I suck! Why does this always happen to me? I am never going to get where I need to be. I'm just not good enough."

Now say to yourself, "HOLD IT! What can I take away that may improve my performance in the future? What is one thing I can change that will help me get where I want to be?"

Here are some examples of radically accepting feedback:

- I'm disappointed with my grade on the test, but I need to put one hour a night into studying from now on.

- I'm hurt that he doesn't want our relationship to continue, but I need to join a book club and running club to get more connected with the world before I date new people.

- I really wanted that job, but I need to start with volunteer experience to build up my resume.

- It was hard to hear that my supervisor thinks my head is not in the job. I need to follow up with a therapist about strategies for managing my ADD.

- My boss has a huge ego, but for me to have an income while I go to law school, I need to make him think the job is my number-one priority.

- My significant other broke up with me because he said I'm lazy. The truth is I need to get at the bottom of why I hold myself back, and I need to do this for me, not for my ex.

Resist self-pity—instead, focus on the problem that is within your control. Of course, you can't control the actions and reactions of others. You do control whether or not you surround yourself with toxic partners and impossible jobs. You also control how much effort you put into your professional pursuits, your psychological well-being, and your physical and emotional health.

When faced with setbacks, remember—self-attack and self-pity breed lethargy and get you nowhere. You can compassionately evaluate yourself, and you can radically accept you need to change to grow. If we aren't taking in feedback and growing, then we are shriveling up and not living life to its fullest.

Learn to Brag

Another important component of reaching goals and managing setbacks is sharing with others what you do feel good about. Women in particular have difficulty being open about their accomplishments and goals. The tendency to not speak confidently about yourself feeds low self-esteem and the sense that your goals are out of reach. The roots of this are present in female socialization and stereotypes.

Through early girlhood experiences, girls are regularly exposed to the disappointing truth that women who do not behave in ways that are consistent with femininity are not as well liked as those who do. For example, women who express anger are seen as less competent than women who adhere to female gender norms and express sadness instead of anger. And women who are assertive may be seen as know-it-alls or bossy. Women tend to downplay their accomplishments and, at least publicly, put out a judicious opinion of themselves to maintain public approval. Many women fear they will be cast out or deemed unacceptable if they do not conform to this implicit girl code.

For example, the bragging female (more so than the bragging male) carries negative connotations. It is common to hear that another female is "too full of herself" or thinks she is "all that." Women are notorious for rolling their eyes at those women who seem too uppity or unapologetically positive about themselves.

There is an important distinction between talking about one's strengths and accomplishments and full-throttle arrogance. For many, however, the threshold for expressing superiority is too low, and they shy away entirely from letting others know their strengths, goals, and ambitions.

Research shows that even when asked to talk about their strengths, women are more likely to endorse or promote other women than themselves. This has far-reaching impacts and, at least in part, plays into why women earn less money than men, are less inclined to negotiate for higher-ranking positions and increased pay, and are generally less comfortable selling themselves for potential opportunities.

Break the Modesty Rule

If you struggle with low self-esteem, then you probably hold back from expressing to others what you are working on improving, what you want in the future, or your career or relationship goals. Not being open about your aspirations means you don't get an opportunity to get help from others, feedback about different approaches, inspiration, or advice. Also, successful people tend to achieve their goals because they think about them, talk about them, and live them out every day. If you are denying yourself the opportunity to be open with others about what you want, then you are less likely to get it.

Challenge female stereotypes that would have you believe something is wrong with a woman speaking confidently about herself. To reduce this type of social anxiety, work to believe that it is not only appropriate but also meaningful to talk about your strengths and accomplishments. *Focus more on getting what you want and talking about what you want. Focus less on what others think of you.*

Provide Your Brain With New Experiences

Genes and experience interact and make a lasting blueprint in the brain by influencing the ways synapses interact. How you know yourself on every level of your existence is represented within the wiring of your brain. When the model for your self-image is negative, the neuronal networks will predictably fire down the same old road of self-doubt and self-criticism. Each new negative thought brings to mind negative thoughts from the past and keeps you in a circular trap. Indeed, for many, these negative-thought streams have been firing for so long that they cue up without a person's conscious awareness.

The process through which one develops low self-esteem (repeatedly feeling criticized and undervalued) is the same process that may undo a negative self-image. It requires repeatedly engaging in new experiences that provide positive feelings. Just like a song you cannot get out of your head, negative-thought streams will replay unless you provide your brain with new experiences. Activating more positive associations of thought will change your brain's wiring and make it easier to cue up positive thoughts and feelings about yourself, even in the presences of defeat and disappointment.

Problem: "I just don't *want* to do it!"
Cure: Do it anyway.

Have you ever had the experience of knowing you should do something while having no desire to do it? Perhaps you know going to the gym, calling a friend, or completing a work assignment will make you feel better about yourself, but you just can't get yourself to act. Maybe you even know that practicing the strategies discussed in this workbook will help you to feel better about yourself. Yet you have no motivation to do so. This occurs because the brain is not an equal-opportunity connector.

The brain has a slight disconnect between thinking and feeling; we may know something to be true and, simultaneously, lack the emotional motivation to do what needs to be done.

Thinking overrides our more primitive base needs all of the time, but this does not occur automatically and requires significant effort. People stop smoking, stop drinking, begin exercising, become parents, quit cheating, become religious, become vegetarian, and undertake any number of other life-altering initiatives. People change all of the time. We all have the capacity to do so. It is a matter of putting in the effort, particularly when trying to develop a new behavior or outlook. You may have to force yourself to go through the motions again and again for months at a time, but you will eventually feel the rewards of your work.

The brain's wiring will remain the same if you keep thinking and experiencing what you have always thought and experienced. On the other hand, if you allow it to do so, the brain has an astonishing ability to adapt and grow in the face of new experience. The remainder of this section addresses new goals and behaviors that, when used with regularity, will reset your self-image.

Exercise: Pick Three Things

A powerful path toward increasing your self-esteem is to put effort into yourself and into what you want out of life, even when it's difficult. Force yourself to do three tasks or chores each day. These are not necessarily pleasurable things—working on yourself takes effort. Straighten up your place, do a load of laundry, cook a meal (or heat up a healthy one), do twenty minutes of vigorous exercise, clean your bathroom(s), call a friend or relative that you have been avoiding, do the rituals of self-care from step three, write in a journal about your thoughts and emotions, or spend ten minutes a day working on the exercises in the Relationship Formula Workbook Series. Force yourself to do these types of tasks even when you don't want to.

Take Bianca as an example. She had profound difficulty investing in herself. She performed well for others—family, work, and friends. But when it came to herself, her home, her physical nutrition and exercise, car repairs, paying bills, or keeping up with chores and errands, she lived in a disorganized and chaotic manner. The more we talked in therapy about self-care, the more Bianca realized how sorely she neglected herself. For a year, she remained resistant to doing anything that was directly nurturing of herself. Then very subtly, over time, she started organizing her home. She began with a drawer a day and, with time, moved up to entire rooms. Eventually this day-by-day work on her home became a gesture of care for herself. She started to feel pride in her home and what she had accomplished and eventually invited people over for social events. When she organized her home, she had more motivation to do laundry and cook meals. Starting with one drawer at time, this home-organization project became a symbol of Bianca taking care of herself and making her own life a priority.

Perhaps it's a struggle for you to take care of yourself unless it involves other people—maybe you go to the gym for your boyfriend and work hard to impress your boss, but when it comes to taking care of yourself for the sake of you, you are at a loss. *Each time you do something for yourself that takes effort, you demonstrate that you are worth the investment.*

Exercise: What Would Life Look Like if You Didn't Feel Bad about Yourself?

Can you imagine how your life would be if you didn't feel badly about yourself, if you did not judge and criticize perceived flaws? Imagine a magic wand passing over you, and suddenly, you no longer have a never-ending list of things you don't like about yourself. The obsessive vigilance about your appearance, personality, intellect, muscle mass, weight, skin, hair, job, finances, and what others think of you are all miraculously gone...and now what? The weight of intrinsic badness you've carried is lifted—you are free. What would your life look like? How would you feel? What would you be doing that you are not currently doing?

Now go back to your "Self-Loathing" list from step one in this workbook. For each item listed (or new ones that come to mind), answer the following questions:

1. If I didn't hate/think/feel _____ about me, then I would be doing _____.

2. If I didn't hate/think/feel_____about me, then I would feel_____.

    Repeat this for as many specific items that come to mind.

Here are some examples: "If I didn't constantly obsess over my weight, I would take more chances getting to know new people"; "If I didn't worry about people liking me, I would feel spontaneous and free to be myself"; "If I didn't feel stupid, I would go back to school and get my master's degree"; or "If I didn't hate my legs, I'd wear more dresses."

Now pick another issue from your self-loathing list, and reflect on the questions above. What would you be doing and feeling if you weren't filled with negative thoughts about yourself? Can you connect with how much holding onto these negative thoughts keeps you stuck and unable to get what you want from life? Most importantly, what is your low self-esteem causing you to miss? Perhaps you would have a better sex life, a more active romantic life, greater emotional intimacy with your friends, a new job, a better school, or a fresh business plan.

Problem: "I don't like the way I look."
Cure: Put active effort into loving the physical you.

It is hard to overemphasize how much people's insecurities about physical appearance can plague them. This is not only true of women but also of men. In my psychotherapy practice, each and every day, half or more of the people I speak with are troubled by their physical appearance. They "hate on" themselves by picking apart each of their perceived flaws. They don't take on new challenges or opportunities. They hold back when meeting new people and generally feel ill at ease and uncomfortable in their own skin. For some, negative feelings about the way they look loom so large that everything else about their personalities has been tamped down. They are unable to experience pleasure, be spontaneous, or generally be themselves.

One of the most damaging aspects of people not accepting their physical appearances is that it invariably impacts their romantic and sex lives. If you're not feeling physically good enough, you may not want to have sex at all. Or you may not enjoy your sexual experiences because you are not fully present in your body during the act. Others have to tune out the actual sex act and instead imagine other people or pornographic images while having sex so as to not feel overly self-conscious.

If you see yourself in this description, stop accepting your dislike of your physical self as the status quo, as something that can't be changed. You have to put in the effort, even though you don't want to, to love your physical self. And I ask you, what is the alternative? Do you want to go through the rest of your days living in a body you despise? Know that people just like you, who focus on working to accept and love themselves, are successful in improving their self-image.

Exercise: Put Active Effort into Loving Your Physical Self

- **Challenge your perceptions about what is physically attractive.** Popular culture promotes a rigid standard of beauty and attraction. While growing up, you were indoctrinated with this standard. In short, you have to look like a celebrity to be desirable or have physical worth. While growing up, you were likely exposed to a range of media—TV, magazines, the Internet, books, pornography—that supported this idea or suggested certain ideals of masculinity and femininity. You may have determined that the idealized look provides a straight path to financial gain, social capital, or true love. Write down what you remember believing about what qualities were attractive for women and men. What was your idea of a beautiful woman and a handsome man? Look at how you feel about attractiveness today. Do you still believe these idealized perceptions are true? If your perceptions are still very similar, perhaps these ideas are limiting in that they represent fantasy versus reality. Can you open up your ideas of attraction and desirability to something less rigid? Ponder examples of attractive people who don't meet popular culture's ideals.

- **Consider your models for self-acceptance:** It's important when growing up to be around people who generally accept both their physical appearances and yours. If you were born into a family that constantly scrutinized weight, or talked about dieting, physical strength, complexions, and hairstyles, then you need a new model for self-acceptance. While you were growing up, were the people you were close to (family, peers, friends, coaches) positive, negative, or neutral about your appearance? Did you hear anything positive about body image from any other male or female in your life? Did you see another female managing weight and her appearance in a healthy manner, not being overly obsessive or self-critical? If the answer to these questions is no, consider how much your view of your own flaws is a repetition of how you saw others treat their physical selves. Perhaps your family unintentionally conditioned you to become hypervigilant about appearance and weight. You can undo this conditioning by noticing when you are obsessing and repeatedly redirecting your attention to other aspects of yourself—your achievements, relationships, activities, and interests.

- **Look yourself in the mirror:** Take off all of your clothing, and look yourself head on in the mirror. Write down in your notebook the automatic thoughts that come to mind. Use the strategies in step two to reframe your automatic thoughts. For example, can you search for the middle path? Try reframing the things you dislike so that they are not overly horrible or unrealistically positive—for example, "My nose is large, but I generally like my face." Work hard, very hard, to find things you can appreciate about your external physical self. Look at yourself, not with your typically critical stance but with kind eyes. Try to appreciate the functionality of your body—what it does for you each and every day. Repeat this exercise every few days to inoculate yourself from your fear of your own image.

- **Learn more about your "lady parts":** Sorry, men. This one is specifically for women. In our current culture, what is promoted as sexy for female genitalia is a kind of rarefied, equally proportioned, odorless, hairless, prepubescent wonder. As a result, many go to great lengths to recreate this pornified image so as to ensure optimal male attraction. They invest money, time, and energy into doctoring up the vulva. The reality is that coiffing and obsessing over the genitalia preoccupies the mind, keeping women from enjoying the actual, in-the-moment sex act. Women who like their intimate parts just as they are and have a working understanding of how their bodies function, not only have higher self-esteem but also tend toward more enjoyment of sex, better sexual functioning, and more routine gynecological visits. If you feel ashamed and disapproving of this part of your body, you are less likely to take care of yourself or enjoy your sex life. In addition, shame leads to self-reconnaissance, which takes you away from experiencing your own sexual desire as distinct from pleasing your partners. For women in particular, a connection with sexual desire has to be consciously built. Spend time working to become more comfortable with your body, all on your own, before you embark on any additional disconnected sexual experiences. Consider reading *Sex Matters For Women*, by Sallie Foley, Sally Kope, and Dennis Sugrue, a guide for further exploring your sexual self.

Problem: "I want to be around others, but then when I am, I want to curl up and be alone."
Cure: Force yourself to bring your full self to the table.

As a psychologist, I talk to people who frequently live double lives. To their friends, families, or spouses, they may seem to have it all together while deep down, they harbor self-doubt, anger, negative thinking, anxiety, or despair. This kind of duality of existence means they never feel quite at home either around people or alone. Around new people, they hold back from being their full and true selves and feel deeply unknown. On the other hand, they are aimless and ill at ease when they are alone.

Opportunities for increasing self-esteem are present in social situations and alone time—the key is to bring your full self to the table in both arenas. Consider taking on the following goals.

Exercise: Become Present

- **Become more alive through authentic connection:** If you are hyper-vigilant about what to say to least offend, and if you perpetually fear how others will judge you, your social connections will be stilted and burdensome. If you are not your real self with others and instead put up walls, then even when you're around people, you will feel alone and misunderstood. As much as possible, when with others, work to be your authentic self by sharing your in-the-moment thoughts, reactions, or feelings. Listen attentively, and react without filtering or self-censoring. Give up the fear of what others will think of you if they learn who you really are and what you really feel. Just as you are not responsible for other people, they are not responsible for you, and the healthy ones will support and listen to you. The benefit of expressing yourself openly far outweighs the minuscule impact of someone having a negative perception or judgment about you.

- **Build close relationships with other women:** This is one more goal specific to women. Research suggests there is one clearly protective element in female development, and that is the power of strong female relationships. Sadly, the rules of femininity and stereotypes about female pettiness can block the development of these powerful relationships. The culture at large stigmatizes women who do not meet current standards of attractiveness, and too often, women use this unforgiving reality to harshly judge other women and to gain leverage and power in female competition. As a result of being treated as if something essential is missing from their physical nature, many women may operate with the belief that other women must be vulnerable to feeling equally deficient. In a world where it seems as if others could turn on you at any time, taking a judgmental stance toward other women is a way to feel a modicum of control. The cost of this tactic is high because harsh judgment and cruelty toward other women is inherently linked to relentless self-scrutiny and panic should one's own flaws be attacked. By judging, fearing, and turning on their own sex, women effectively self-sabotage their opportunities for strong female relationships and greater empowerment. And in this environment, a woman may begin to believe that other women are untrustworthy, paving the way to more alienation. The more girls and women can stay connected to their actual experiences and engage less with the rigid expectations of others, the greater will be their empathy and compassion for other women who may be bound by these same rigid expectations. Challenge your ideas about women being "petty," "gossipy," or "untrustworthy." See if this has more to do with how you see yourself versus the true, inherent nature of women. Accept that these stereotypes limit you from getting the kind of care and support that can be deeply impactful in your journey toward feeling good enough.

- **Reduce your time on social media:** Many with low self-esteem turn to social media in an attempt to feel better about themselves. At first, social media offers a safe way to connect—you don't actually have to go into a new situation, and you can engage the world from the comfort of your couch; you don't have to share anything you don't wish the world to know, and you can put your most positive self-image forward. The reality is, for some, social-media sites become sources of endless self-comparison—where a person with low self-esteem does not have to look far to find someone who appears to have it better. Whether it's a better body, higher-achieving children, a hotter girlfriend, more impressive academic accomplishments, or sexier vacations, there is plenty of material on social-media sites to support a negative self-appraisal. Do people really need any more fodder for feeling poorly about themselves? After all, in the United States, twenty million women are believed to suffer from full-blown eating disorders. And girls as young as six express concerns about their body image. By elementary school, 40 to 60 percent of girls say they worry about becoming too fat, a concern that once established stays with them for the rest of their lives. And over the last ten years, the number of men diagnosed with eating disorders has steadily increased. More men are finding themselves obsessed with thinness and physical perfection. Research shows a relationship between social comparison, depressive symptoms, and Facebook usage. If you overuse social media and are negatively comparing yourself, your life, your body, and your accomplishments to others, then you are engaging in repetitive negative thoughts about yourself. Negatively comparing yourself to others on social-media sites only increases a sense that you will never be good enough in your real, day-to-day life.

- **Book your time:** New research suggests that the lonely brain is already in a distressed state when entering social situations. So if you have a tendency to isolate and then you are thrown into a social event, you are actually more likely to perceive the people present as negative or threatening toward you. If you are accustomed to being around people, your brain is less distressed when you walk into social situations, and you feel less social anxiety. Force yourself each week to book two to three activities where you are around others and engaging in conversation. The more you do it, the less threatening and difficult it will be. On the other hand, isolating yourself puts you in limbo—you feel lonely, and yet you avoid socializing. The more you book your time and regularly keep those commitments, the less emotionally burdensome social events and people will become. Eventually, you will feel less lonely and more connected.

- **Search for peaceful solitude each day (even if only for a few moments):** Being comfortable alone goes hand in hand with being at ease with others. This is because we radiate to others the feelings we carry in our bodies. This radiance can often set the theme for how our interactions will go. If you are always busy, frazzled, and never at peace, others pick up this frenetic energy and will not be at peace with you in your presence. If you carry habitual sadness or anger, those you want to connect with will feel these emotions in your presence. Work to find moments where you can connect with yourself, without obsessively thinking about your flaws, the flaws of others, or what needs to be done next. Look for moments when you can concentrate on purposeful breathing and observing your thought streams, emotional states, and physical sensations. Meditating goes far when it comes to dealing with others in your life. Resolve to connect with a peaceful feeing inside your own body, and you will begin to extend this composure to all of your interactions. Being self-possessed will help you to appreciate others, stay in the present, and even transfer to them the same sense of well-being.

- **Build up roles and responsibilities for yourself—separate from your relationships:** For some, when they are not around others, their internal light fades into darkness, and they have no sense of who they are or what to do with themselves. The more you accomplish and the more complicated your sense of self is, the higher your self-esteem. Don't put everything on the guy, the girl, the job, the kid—think about yourself multidimensionally. Consider new professional, academic, or volunteer roles that you can take on—all on your own. Knowing you have a variety of ways to contentedly fill your time will help you to feel less vulnerable when your friendships or romantic partners let you down.

- **Let yourself live alone for a period of time:** I talk to people sixty and older who say they regret that they got married or partnered up so early in life. One woman said, "I wish I would have taken the opportunity in my twenties to live alone and get used to myself because now I'm terrified about what to do on my own, and yet I deeply crave it at the same time." Take these opportunities, whether you're between relationships, divorced, young, or old. Take whatever opportunity you can to live on your own for a period of time. Allow yourself to deeply root into being you and into being comfortable with you.

Final Note

Change is possible, and a change in how you view yourself, more than any potential future relationship, will impact the most important part of your existence—your ability to be present in the here and now. The more present you can be and the less wracked by anxious fears and self-doubt, the more you can enjoy every aspect of this life—right now.

Summary of the Five Steps

Step	Action to take
#1: Take stock of what you won't accept about yourself.	Stop avoiding yourself and all you don't like about yourself—this only perpetuates your low self-esteem. Identify the connection between your internal critic and external factors— your past experiences or the ways other people treat you—that contributes to you feeling poorly about yourself.
#2: Connect with the eye of your storm.	What you think about and how you think about yourself impact how good or bad you feel. Identify your automatic thoughts and core beliefs. Use the *thought inventory* to cut off negative-thinking spirals before they make you feel unworthy.
#3: Radically accept.	Identify what destructive behaviors you have implemented to cope with not liking yourself. Start entirely accepting yourself as you are while also taking better care of yourself through *humanizing your internal critic* and *daily rituals of self-love.*
#4: Change your approach to setbacks.	View yourself as a person in progress. You are not at the mercy of life; take responsibility for what can be changed, and compassionately accept that which cannot. Be open with others about your strengths and areas of growth.
#5: Provide your brain with new experiences.	Increase your self-esteem *now* by behaviorally confronting all that you have avoided. Put effort into investing in yourself through forcing yourself to engage in new, real-life social, sexual, and emotional experiences.

What Is the Relationship Formula?

*B*uilding Self-Esteem is part of the Relationship Formula Workbook Series, four brief workbooks designed to help people who struggle with relationships. Whether you are married, single, divorced, newly starting your dating life—and whether you're gay or straight—this workbook series will increase your relationship preparedness so that you may better find healthy, meaningful partnership.

As a psychologist, I see people who talk about feeling they are "emotionally flawed" or "incapable of finding healthy love," or they describe a history of dating "losers" or a series of chronically disappointing relationships. They say they have "repetitive relationship issues" and fear they will never crack the code for love and romance, telling me they've "never had a real relationship" or beating themselves up with laments like "What is wrong with me that I can't get what seems so easy for everyone else?"

If you can't get relationships right, constantly feel as if something is wrong with you when it comes to romance, and/or find you are continually drawn to the same kinds of disappointing or dysfunctional partners, then the Relationship Formula Workbook Series offers a way to gain control. Before you pick your next romantic partner, give yourself an opportunity to be all you can be—because that process will help you find all you deserve.

People who struggle with feeling good enough to get what they want out of life or those who have a history of unfulfilling relationships typically benefit from learning new skills. These four workbooks cover managing four key areas of growth:

1. *Breaking Up & Divorce 5 Steps: How to Heal and Be Comfortable Alone*
2. *Building Self-Esteem 5 Steps: How to Feel "Good Enough" about Yourself*
3. *Toxic Love 5 Steps: How to Identify Toxic-Love Patterns* and *Find Fulfilling Attachments*
4. *Getting Close to Others 5 Steps: How to Develop Intimate Relationships and Still Be True to Yourself*

Many who struggle with relationships alternate between self-blame for not "getting it right" or inflating and romanticizing what they think others have that they can't get. The statistics on marital abuse, distress, and infidelity paint a different picture. Many marriages are based on unhealthy relationship patterns of codependency, avoidance, living entirely separate lives, and in some cases, emotional abuse. Half of marriages result in divorce, and more than half of second marriages result in divorce. Even couples who stay together for a lifetime aren't necessarily happy or healthy. The reality is relationships take work, and even people who are married or appear to have it all have not always done the necessary work.

The Relationship Formula is not about telling you whom to date; rather, it focuses on the one part of romance that you can control—yourself.

The impact relationships, in particular romantic ones, have on our lives cannot be overstated. They influence physical health, psychological well-being, professional success, lifespan, pleasure, and the emotional success of our children or future children. When you decide working on yourself is a priority, you are taking a step that will powerfully influence the trajectory of most aspects of your life. This change has the potential to ripple out to every relationship—close friendships, parents, siblings, nieces, nephews, work colleagues, and classmates, as well as children born and unborn. By building yourself up, you acquire the capacity to build others up.

Relationships have the power to heal, to connect and to provide immeasurable warmth to buffer life's harshest realities. On the flip side, destructive relationships are also powerful and can do crushing harm. You have the ability to choose which path you take. If you decide to take this one—that is, building yourself up from the inside out—work on believing with every fiber of your being that if you persevere, life will get better.

The Relationship Formula Workbook Series is designed to be used on your own or together with a therapist. Oftentimes, working with a therapist can be tremendously effective in understanding yourself and building more positive patterns of interacting. For others, going to therapy requires more money or time than they have. Some simply prefer to do this work on their own. However you approach the work is okay, provided persistence rules.

This program is modular with four separate workbooks. Some may wish to go through all four. Others will prefer to tailor their approach to their specific histories and issues. It is absolutely fine to complete one workbook or to go forth and complete all four in any order. As you read through the steps, you may come up with your own strategies or find idiosyncratic ways to combine various tools to suit your personality or personal struggle. Keep a notebook of your work so you can review what you have written down and have learned about yourself as you grow through this program. The more you review the material, the more the tools described will become automatic.

The work may seem daunting at first, but what is far harder is a lifetime of frustrating and disappointing attempts at securing love. Just like beginning a new physical exercise program, it's difficult initially but with time, the routine becomes easier and easier. You will notice progress, begin to feel better, and have more positive interactions with others. These rewards will reinforce, and day by day, you will grow.

Made in the USA
Middletown, DE
12 February 2018